The Essence
Of My Totality

Volume Two

The Writer's Edition

The Essence
Of My Totality

Volume Two
The Writer's Edition

La Toya T. Robinson

LTR Unlimited

Somerville, Massachusetts

THE ESSENCE OF MY TOTALITY

Volume Two The Writer's Edition

By LaToya T. Robinson

Published by: LTR Unlimited

Toyat143@gmail.com

La Toya T. Robinson, Publisher / Editorial Director

Caryn Hirsch, Graphic Design/ Cover Design

Jack Rummel Photography, cover photos

Yvonne Rose/Quality press info, Book Packager

LTR Unlimited Books are available at special discounts for bulk purchases, sales promotions, fundraising or educational purposes.

ISBN# 978-0-9967045-0-2

For all those who have chosen to stick by

my side through this amazing journey

called life; you are, and always will be,

what's important.

Thank You

So, it's been 5 years...

Since, The Essence of My Totality, Volume One was released.

So much has happened in my life since then,

so much change; which is good.

My life, like all of our lives, has been altered by experience.

I'm growing, shifting, and changing more and more each day.

As I mentioned in the intro to my first volume;

I'm not very good at being vocal about my emotions.

Therefore, writing is the way I express myself best;

poetry specifically.

As a child I always kept a diary.

I would pour out my heart on each page.

It was full of my thoughts on life

and detailed my escapades; on a daily basis.

Writing about what was going on around me,

and happening to me, allowed me, at a young age,

to learn to keep everything in perspective.

I haven't looked at them in a long while,

but if I did;

I'm sure I would laugh and cry

at the good times and bad times

that made up my childhood and general upbringing.

As I grew, the format began to change, as the format of my life did.

During my early college years I stopped keeping a journal, but I didn't stop writing.

One day,

I sat back with one of my many notebooks

and realized

it was full of melody.

The transition was naturally seamless;

one I didn't even recognize was happening.

My mode of expression changed,

and since then I've continued to hone that change.

That change was,

and still is to this day

a very important part of who I am.

It always will be.

My writing is deeply emotional.

I rarely sit down to write with a true ending in mind.

When I grab a pen and paper

(or these days my phone with a little

help from my Microsoft Office app)

it's because I feel compelled from within to put them to use.

My poetry is my diary, and sharing isn't easy.

However,

over the years,

I've felt compelled to share with those I'm close to

. I've also written poems for those I'm not close to,

but whom my spirit felt

would benefit from the power of my words.

Words are strong.

Communication is important.

Therefore,

though it is hard for me to share certain work,

I felt compelled to organize this volume

based on my love for writing,

and what the process of creating does for my soul.

It is my hope that through my words

others will be moved to do

whatever it is their souls compel them to do too.

So, thank you,

for taking the time to read and hear these words;

words written to tap into your emotions and motivate you spirit.

Peace and Love,

La Toya T. Robinson

Table of Contents

Foreword

LaToya embodies a litany of adjectives, daughter, sister, aunt, artist, educator; however, the adjective that captures her wholeness is- HUMAN. Her innate ability to find humanity in the most futile of places and to conjure the good in humanity in the bowels of despair is humanly Ms. LaToya T. Robinson. Her life's work and the words on the pages that will precede these will empower some and enable others; however, they will not be devoid of a human spirit that is committed to unapologetically illicit a paradigm shift in one's present station in life.

As the world's students continue to allow themselves to be trapped by the manacles of narcissism better known as social media it misses opportunities to get lost in words that are honest, vulnerable, and humanly accessible. LaToya simultaneously provides you with an escape while gifting you with a spiritual journey of the Human Ethos. The Essence of My Totality -- Volume 2: The Writers Edition will be one of your most important reads as it will help you release a variance of emotions while empowering you to dream without limits. Open it and begin to re-connect with your humanness.

Tony Clark

A Scribe's Release

I do not

do what I do

for recognition.

I do what I do,

because,

my soul is on a mission.

To release

the unknown from

deep down.

Truthfully.

Right now.

I'd rather be asleep.

For some,

that's the enemy.

For me,

that's peace.

Peace of mind.

Piece of Me.

Peace

for progress

and solemnity.

Peace to dream.

For peace and serenity.

So,

Let me repeat.

I do not

do what I do

for recognition.

I do what I do,

because,

my mind is on a mission.

To release strange thoughts, that

keep me apart

from those

around me.

Or,

maybe they just seem strange;

because really,

2

I have changed.

But,

my roots remain the same.

All I've been through

will always

be a part of me.

Truthfully.

Right now.

I'd rather be chilling.

Just really

not caring what the

world

or people in it think

about me.

To an extent,

I don't.

but,

When it comes to the people I love,

It matters the most.

To make them proud

is my goal.

That goal

alters the way I function.

Puts my soul

in conjunction

with my mind.

Enhances my grind;

which again,

initiates changes

in how I operate.

I'm always shifting,

growing,

Rearranging,

Yet, maintaining balance.

So,

I'll say it one last time.

I do not

do what I do

for recognition.

I do what I do

Because,

my spirit is on a mission,

To never allow downtime,

Steadily remain

clandestine.

Until I'm ready,

to let the cadence in my

voice reveal my truth.

To

spew no lies.

Recognition comes to me.

without necessity to seek it out.

I do

what I do

for the peace it gives me.

And I'll always do

what I do,

No matter who knows me.

A/V

I'm a

visual girl,

in an

audio world.

So,

I speak my words to be heard,

as I see them,

on a scroll in my mind.

I speak clearly

one syllable at a time.

I try to

design a scene

that will make you scream,

from your soul

'til you cry.

Like,

when the one you love

fills you deep inside.

Now,

visualize that.

Hear the sounds

from the back.

Listen real close.

Do you see it?

I bet.

The sweat. The wet.

Are you feeling me yet?

I'm just a visual girl,

in an audio world.

So,

I spew my words

to be heard.

Entice your intellect

with nouns and verbs.

Grasp your emotions with

paradoxical terms.

Like,

Are you in love?

Or filled with hate?

Are you at peace?

Or ready for war?

Where you going?

Heaven or hell?

Go ahead,

I'll give you a chance to

think more.

So,

to my audio world,

you've got this girl,

who came to visualize,

then vocalize,

to give you

what you came for.

Changes

Change,

is a constant topic in my writing.

Change,

is necessary

to continue fighting;

through

life's constant barrage of situations.

Frustration at times,

Takes over our minds,

And change,

is yet to be a thought.

Instead,

we dream of ways to change the day,

Without thoughts of

the bigger picture.

And an understanding

of the fact that

complacency

is a quicker killer of the soul.

Self-restoration

is never

self-deprecating;

because that type of change

is for the best.

Those around you will

never understand,

Until,

they see your happiness expand.

When they see you've shaken off

all the loose ends

that once held you down.

Sometimes this takes,

change of mind,

change of friends,

Maybe a change outbound;

beyond your comfort zone.

To a place

your heart condones

as right.

Some search all their lives.

Some give up

before they arrive;

when any good change would

have allowed them to carry on.

Change,

is a constant topic in my writing

because I know.

Some small and large changes,

MAY rearrange us,

But WILL make us stronger

as we grow.

Free Write

While my mind moves,

a mile a minute.

I try to pinpoint

one thought.

I can't.

But,

my pen is fluid.

Picking up,

the thoughts

that were chopped.

I try to keep

the stream straight,

across the page,

like it's supposed to be.

But,

I couldn't do that naturally.

The lines,

they make me feel trapped.

You see,

I have a small problem

with authority.

But, my words,

you understand fluently.

Where am I going with this?

Be patient please.

Work with me.

I'm free writing

with my pen.

Who is a

real close friend.

You think I'm crazy, because

it's inanimate.

But,

what it represents,

is

my weapon.

My tool

to create my essence.

I Indulge My Passions

I indulge my passions,

in a fashion

most others don't.

But,

less seldom than those

who don't know how

to draw a line.

A line

which is

quite fine, but still

real,

all the same.

Balance is key.

Light within the darkness

and

shade within the light

are always viable

possibilities.

My life

has been lived consistently on the

precipice of two sides.

Two worlds that will

never collide.

Two worlds,

side by side;

in which,

I

hurdle,

straddle,

or stand on either side of.

Never choosing either one.

Always searching

for proper footing.

Which is necessary;

in a life indulged

by passions.

Equilibrium becomes

an action

so complacency

does not.

Art

is a great distraction,

no matter where I reside.

A portrait of words

vertically placed.

Otherwise,

I

consistently build supplies

right beside the line

at either side,

in case

I need to make

a quick decision.

But,

if you look real close,

you will see,

there is a

small incision,

right on the line READY

to engulf my supplies for

when

I decide

to stream.

Choose one route, instead

of

dancing about waiting

for one to choose me.

My passions are intense. I

know.

I live

With

Intent to grow;

nonetheless.

So,

I indulge my passions,

in a fashion

most others don't.

But,

less seldom

than those

who don't know

how to draw a line.

A line,

which is quite fine,

but still real,

all the same.

No Negativity Necessary

It feels like,

I haven't written

in a while.

I've been

spending

a lot of time

with a

brand new smile.

One that's relaxed,

yet,

wide,

from ear to ear.

And,

it's clear to see,

I'm changing.

Maintaining

who I am inside.

Rearranging

the aura

of negativity

that had once arrived.

Replacing it

with

a positive tone.

Upholding a life

my heart condones.

Persuading my urges

to cease and desist.

And,

urging my mind

to persist.

To pursue

an enlightened longevity.

With

no negativity necessary.

Purity

Sometimes,

I feel like,

I'm trying to rhyme harder

then I should be.

When I know

my words flow

more like poetry.

In my mind,

I try to find,

peace,

serenity.

I let my words

represent this entity,

of my soul.

To take control

of your attention.

Not to mention,

your heart.

As my words flow.

like a stream,

You dream

I want to be able

to create

a scene,

in your mind.

That way,

I'll know my words

are divine,

because,

sometimes,

a sweet serene syllable

is so hard to find.

So,

I write

to create.

I write

to get away.

I write

to stay sane.

I write

every day.

When I don't,

I begin to feel lost

That's when

I try to rhyme

all hard.

But,

I'm no hardcore gangster.

I'm soft and discreet.

And I enjoy

writing lines,

of pure poetry.

Pushing Through the Barricade

I feel a writer's block,

'cause the

music is hot.

Takin' my mind,

away from what I'm assigned.

It ain't homework though,

so,

I can take it slow,

when I write for myself.

I could never

leave my mind

locked in a cell.

The way some people do.

Not letting their

dreams come true.

Please!

I know what I have to do.

First,

I have to get over

this hump

of negativity.

Haters,

who love me.

But,

hate so much,

they can't see.

My spirit is pumping

with high-powered energy.

There's no stopping me. My possibilities are endless.

I feel like an ant, trying to learn

the world's geography.

Not far off though,

I see my way through.

So,

I'll continue chasing my dreams,

in full hot pursuit

And.

when the time is up?

I hope I'm not overdue.

I'll be ready,

To make all

my dreams come true.

Questions?

What do you do

when you feel you've lost the fight?

Regroup the troops?

Strengthen the lines?

Decide your re-approach;

late into the night?

What do you do

when you feel you've lost your might?

When all you wanted,

and all you need,

ceased to be

the exact same thing.

Reprioritize?

No longer wear a disguise,

to hide,

that you know,

what you're searching for

just maybe hard to find.

And when it's found;

how do you keep it?

What do you do when retention

is a threat just to mention?

What do you do?

How do you move?

Hold it all in until fully consumed?

All these questions,

are deep in my mind.

But,

dealing with emotions

tends to

hamper my grind.

So,

at least I ask the questions.

It's a good place to start.

To contemplate my mental

state.

Leave my mind open to elevate,

and ease the burden

on my heart.

What do I do,

while these questions

flood my mind?

I,

Let the stream flow,

allow my passions to rise,

pick up a pen and paper,

emotionally strategize,

so

my soul can take control

and

have the power to decide.

See

Let's see,

Where do I begin?

How do I proceed?

When my heart is heavy,

and I need to plead,

but no one is around to hear

me speak;

so,

I pull out a pen,

and let my heart bleed.

See,

I feel like Drake did,

In that song "Over",

wondering,

"where did all these people come from?"

When last year

I had no idea

about any of them.

And the ones I thought

I did know and love;

Fell short with support

when THEY thought I hit

one level above.

You see,

to them,

I wasn't there like before.

But,

my dreams take work.

my life changed for the

score;

I've just been,

trying to reach.

Been trying breach.

Refusing to stop,

Refusing a seat.

Standing tall;

not weak,

Just refusing defeat.

See,

In life,

I've been taught some real silly things.

Listening to

experiences and taking advice,

from people who thought

I should listen up

twice

to what life and trials

and focus could bring.

Until I realized,

those things were for them;

not me.

Mostly about men,

and what it took to be,

A good lover,

A good girlfriend,

A good partner,

A good wife,

A good friend.

I listened.

I cared for each word.

Even when

I was told the absurd.

Like,

How I should never ever care.

And so,

I never dared.

And,

how I should learn to share,

Because there are good men

who can care

for two hearts at one time.

And so,

I tried.

And I found out,

all that shit was a lie.

Then,

any good man I found,

didn't trust me an ounce.

They just couldn't understand how,

If I'm so smart,

I would think any of that shit would work out.

So, now you see,

here I am,

Just as alone as can be,

With all these people

around who think they

know me.

So,

I put my knees to the

ground,

and one hand in the air.

I pray to the Lord,

that He always be there.

To watch over me,

as I follow my dreams,

'cause I know if I don't,

I won't get any sleep,

and sleep's what I need for my

productivity.

I ask

that He gives me love and faith.

A love that comes with no

judgment or haste.

I ask

that He keep my heart true because

I just don't know how

to be fake.

If I don't care,

You know it.

If I love you,

I show it.

But I've learned

That's rare in the people I meet.

So,

I ask that He,

Send me people

Whose hearts are true.

This loneliness hurts,

but I'll make it through.

I'm wise enough to know;

I've hurt people too.

And what comes around

goes around;

I'm paying my dues.

So,

I finally figured out,

where to begin.

The question remains.

Now where do I end?

Sit

Sitting down to write

isn't usually

the way I do things.

It's a subconscious spontaneity.

When I need time to breath,

I just let my right hand move,

fancy techniques.

Which allow me

to speak,

candidly.

No fantasies of how I wish things could be.

Just about what I see

in front of me.

But today,

I sit to write

No particular end in sight.

Just

ensuring my need to feel alive.

My right hand

keeps me balanced.

Balanced

outside the lines.

The ones

designed

to keep people confined.

Sitting down to write

isn't usually

the way I do things.

My decision to write

truly isn't

a decision at all.

It's my

innate reaction

when nature calls.

I can't ignore it.

Nor do I try.

Resistance is futile

when

caught in the wild,

and this page

is my everglades.

My way of stalking prey.

Today I sit to write.

My soul has so much to unload.

I need some way to

let it go

at high decibel tones.

Leaving my mind free

to roam

through the jungle.

It's a blank page to you,

but to me,

it's full of wonders.

Wild and dangerous.

Screaming to express

the depths

of my soul's frustrations.

Patiently waiting to pounce

and strike out of hiding.

I never sit to write,

but right now, I'm excited.

It's inspiring.

This is my transition time.

Transition is consistent in my life.

Change is what I crave.

Constantly I feel caged

by monotony.

I've always believed

switching things up

led to what life

should be.

And so,

As I dwell deep in my wilderness,

I fight

through the maze of my minds mental abstracts.

Attacking line after line.

My right hand guides my tracks.

Today I sat to write.

Today I decided to fight.

Today I decided to live.

Today I will follow

the path my right hand

has laid out,

with no doubts.

Today I sat to write.

In vain?

Possibly.

But,

when I don't write,

I'm blind,

walking aimlessly about.

And so

Today I sat to write

Which usually

isn't the way I do things.

True Creativity

Putting the pen to paper.

Not sure,

what I have to say.

It always happens this way.

I've barely

been able to write,

with thoughts lingering.

I organize my mind,

when I see

the ink cross the line.

It's quite a fine feeling,

when you see a project

in continuous progression.

Not sure,

where it began,

or where it will stop.

That's passion.

That's fire

burning hot.

Pure art.

Quite possibly,

the most beautiful thing.

Spewing out,

naturally flowing.

Unforced, and

constantly growing.

The feeling of not knowing.

What's coming next?

The question

keeps it going.

The mystery to see,

what was once unforeseen.

It's an unbelievable scene.

Putting the pen to paper.

What can I create?

The possibilities are endless.

Superfluous,

is the thought to wait,

hesitate,

and loose something

that might have been great.

When I Write

Lately,

I've been at a loss

for words.

Not writing much.

This shit is absurd.

Unheard of,

and it gets on my nerves.

When I write,

I fight for my pride.

I fight with my soul.

Stories in my mind,

begin to unfold.

Untold thoughts form,

and,

rearrange in a rage.

Quick,

incomplete,

I fill the meat on the page.

When I write,

I fight

with what's real,

and what's not.

Creating pure art;

for the masses to receive.

When I write,

I fight

for the artist in me.

When I write.

My mind sets in flight;

I journey to far off lands.

My escapades withstand

re-writes with my pen.

They come from

my journey within.

And,

that's alright.

Late at night.

At home,

when I write.

Why I Love Poetry

Why do I love poetry?

Because,

it's always been with me,

Throughout the deep

insecurities,

that have lingered

throughout my life.

Why do I love poetry?

Because,

It's how you notice me.

At least,

that's what I thought,

the first time

I was

inspired to read

the things I write.

Why do I love poetry?

Because,

I've always been spoiled,

see,

With materialistic

non-necessities,

And my deepest emotions

abandoned,

way out to sea.

I began to write

to enhance my life;

showing those closest

my innate light.

Poetry glows

deep within my sights.

Keeps my eyes wide and bright;

despite the need to fight

outside entities.

Those that tell me,

I can't be.

Those who have no faith in me.

Why do I love poetry?

Because,

It holds me closely;

day and night.

When my words grow tight,

My emotions flow,

And my soul thinks slow.

To entice my

effervescence outside.

Hopefully,

You will see

why I love this art.

Why poetry is smart

for those like me.

People who have the tendency

to hold it all inside

For those who are

afraid to cry

with someone sitting

by their side.

Poetry

takes a hold of me.

And so,

I give in totally.

Then wait…

until

it explodes from me!

That feeling

is why I love poetry.

It completes my life.

Writer's Block

Suffering,

from some kind of writer's

block.

Suffering,

from a mind that's numb

with thoughts,

of getting ahead.

My head

has been laced.

I can feel the stress,

in my

midbrain, forebrain,

others can see it in my face.

A disgrace,

to what I've always

planned to be.

An endless beauty.

Instead,

there are lines and bags.

Signs of a hag,

But,

still I'm young.

I hate to be blasé.

But,

"don't young girls,

just wanna have fun?"

I guess

that's just after

knowing,

what you're doing in life.

Well,

I've decided what I am.

A writer.

Who doesn't

take enough time,

to write.

Instead,

I fight and I fight,

with my ego.

I try to hold back

my pride.

I try not

to be boastful.

Or,

show my emotions

on the outside.

Because,

when I feel high,

others let their spirit die.

They say,

it's because

of a

pure conceit in me.

But,

I've just never been

bashful,

or,

good with defeat.

All my issues,

come from empathy.

Feeling so much for

another,

you take on their emotions.

This should never be

confused with, your true

devotions.

Somehow, I found myself

caught in this web.

Finding it hard

to unwind,

and,

get myself ahead.

Confidence is the attribute

I try to exude.

Not conceit.

Not being judgmental,

or treating other

people cheap.

So,

Can I please be me?

And we,

as a people must see,

no matter what

we may think,

showing our envy,

makes us weak.

About the Author

La Toya T. Robinson is a poet, educator, and personality. As a poet, La Toya's debut publication was self-published, "The Essence of My Totality" - Volume One, which contains uplifting poetry to positively motivate your spirit.

As an educator, La Toya is a Program Director at Bunker Hill Community College, and is a Theater Arts Educator who created A Step Beyond theater program in conjunction with Boston's Centers for Youth and Families.

As a personality, Ms. Toya Tiffany has previously worked as a radio personality for WERS, HOT97Boston, and Boston's Underground Radio.

La Toya straddles the worlds of both education and the arts, as she believes they are connections to knowledge and culture and helps create bridges for the next generation.

ORDER FORM

Please Contact

La Toya T. Robinson

LTR Unlimited at toyat143@gmail.com

Please send_____copy(ies) of *The Essence of My Totality Volume Two, The Writers Edition* _____

Name/Address:_____

City:_____State:_____Zip: _____

Telephone: (   )_____ / (   )_____

Email: _____ _____

I have enclosed $18.73, plus $3.00 shipping per book for a total of

$_____.

Sales Tax: Add 6.75% to total cost of books for orders shipped to MA addresses.

For Bulk or Wholesale Rates, Email: Toyat143@gmail.com

For further information about this book or for appearances, you can reach La Toya Robinson: Toyat143@gmail.com

www.ingramcontent.com/pod-product-compliance
Lightning Source LLC
Chambersburg PA
CBHW060427090426
42734CB00011B/2480